# LITTL
# BIG LOVE

## 50 Ways to Express and Acknowledge Love with Words

For Melissa,
    Love is everywhere
always. Always look
for love and always
find love!

        David

# LITTLE BOOK OF
# BIG LOVE

## 50 Ways to Express and
## Acknowledge Love with Words

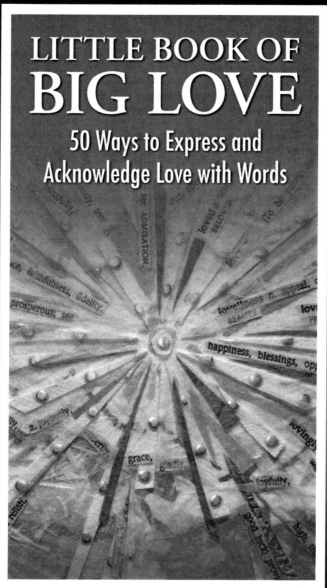

# DAVID LAZAROFF

**Little Book of Big Love – 50 Ways to Express and Acknowledge Love with Words**

Copyright © 2013 By David Lazaroff
Published by Expressionist Press LLC
Denver, Colorado
www.expressionistpress.com
877-926-9300

ISBN 13: 978-0-9851631-0-5

# DEDICATION

To
my family.
You introduce me to a way of love
that I cherish.

To
Meredith, my wife.
You show me colors of love
I cannot imagine.

To
Gurumayi Chidvilasananda.
You give your life so that others
may experience eternal love every day.

To
you.
You give the effort to notice
the presence of love and
share your experience.
You make life beautiful for all of us.

# ACKNOWLEDGEMENTS

L ove is an experience of sharing. It is impossible to name each person who has taught me of love, because everyone is a unique expression of love and every expression contributes to me and this book whether I am aware of it or not. Certainly, I have many lessons in love from my wife, Meredith, my parents, my sisters, my cousins, and my in-laws and all my extended family.

Here I acknowledge a few of the many individuals who interacted with me directly on the effort of creating the pages of this book.

Wendy Talley and Marilyn Patton contribute their expressions of love. Comments and feedback are contributed by Tina Stille, Christina Surretsky, Michelle Marison, Andrea Adler, Melissa Chaney, Brandy Sarasvati, Audrey Dockins, Christine Parasmo, Camille Ibsen, Mary Schauer, and Nichole Douglas.

I acknowledge Amber Ocean for the contribution of the cover artwork. Amber, you are an ocean of love.

I acknowledge Mary Ann Tate for her editing, feedback and partnership in reaching out to readers to spread love.

I acknowledge Ivan Jungé for his contribution of graphic design, typesetting, feedback, and willingness to play and contribute.

# CONTENTS

# INTRODUCTION

An ancient text from India known as The Bhakti Sutras says, "The nature of love cannot be defined." In light of this statement, it is no wonder that people sometimes experience frustration when expressing their experience of love, acknowledging the love of another, or understanding another's experience of love. One source of this frustration is the contrast between the few ways our culture gives us to express love with words and the infinite ways in which love is manifest in the world.

I suggest that the root of the problem is that we are too close to love to see it clearly as something "out there" to be distinguished as separate from ourselves or objects in the world. Consider that a fish, born deep in the ocean, never to be out of the water, cannot distinguish wet from dry. The fish has no point of reference for contrast.

So, I ask you to consider the possibility that we live in a Universe that is made entirely of the primary element of love. This element might be known in physics as the Higgs boson or the Higgs field with properties that might be described as "affinity". It is theorized that it is the Higgs boson that gives other particles mass and the Higgs field exists everywhere always. The possibility of mass makes manifestation possible.

Further, consider if the entire Universe is manifest in patterns of affinity. From sub-atomic particles to minerals to plants to humans to cities and social structures, all that exists has a degree of workable interaction. I assert this workable interaction may be looked upon as a degree of affinity or love. Where workability is absent, the unworkable falls out of existence and becomes extinct.

In such a construction, the instruments of perception and that which is observed are of the same essence and cannot detect their commonality any more than you or I can detect the color of our eyes without a reflection or an outside observer.

Suppose, also, that the nature of this love expresses, or manifests, itself in the form of patterns that call forth an experience of connectedness, harmony, and recognition. Really, I suggest that this is Self-recognition of the primary element: Love.

So, what does this say about our experience of love? What does such a viewpoint make available? This point of view is consistent with the experiences of connectedness, unity, self-recognition, affinity, and beauty associated with what we call love. This view invites us to look for the pattern expression of love in everyone and everything.

As you look for the expression of love in the world with the understanding that love is what the world is made of, you become more adept at recognizing it and experiencing the joy of love!

Please, give this the practice and patience it deserves. You deserve love. Love is your birthright.

In these pages I offer you starting points to use words to explore the nature of love. Please take what I offer and modify and mold it to be your own expression. Write your personal expression or acknowledgement in the space provided. Express love as you recognize it arising from within. Explore love as you see love expressing itself through others. Celebrate love as you experience love with another.

# Expressing Your Love For Another

You feel love. There it is in your body. How does it show up this time? Does your heart beat quicker? Does your stomach tense? Do your shoulders relax? The feelings you have are measurable body sensations with distinct physiology and chemistry. It is not well understood how these feelings work or shift, yet it is undeniable that you experience them. These feelings don't come with a manual describing their meaning, expected duration, and how to best integrate them into your life. You are the manual and you choose what the feelings mean.

Love is your experience. You notice that when in the presence of a particular person, an experience of love arises within you. You notice that you have love for another. When you notice the experience of love, you may also notice that other feelings, opinions, and thoughts might not be displaced by the love. Yes, many feelings can co-exist. Yes, you may have these feelings for many people. There is no limit.

The love manifesting in your body may want to be shared and expressed to others. This is not always the case, so listen closely to the love arising within you. Words may be a very powerful and appropriate means for expressing your love for another. Here I offer you a few options to try out. Bend them to your liking and mold them to be authentic for you. Write your own expression in the available space.

Express love for the joy of the expression. I suggest you set aside the expectations for a response and pay close attention to expressing your true feelings. It is one experience to have love within you and a completely new experience of that love when it is expressed to another. Does the feeling dissipate? Does the feeling grow? Does the expression fall flat? Any way it goes, don't attach too much meaning to it. Every expression is unique in relation to the people involved, the time, and the place of expression. Just notice if the expression is helpful or not, **this time**. Then, move on or stay with it, whichever works for your life and relationships.

Your love is a gift to the world that only you can deliver. Thank you for being willing to give it.

## Internet Bonus!

David's suggestions for gifts when you want to express your love for another with more than words:

www.LittleBookOfBigLove.com/express

Share your expressions of love:

www.LittleBookOfBigLove.com/share

Get weekly tips on expressing and acknowledging love:

www.LittleBookOfBigLove.com/tips

## *I love you.*

The phrase "I love you" is so overused that too often when we rely on it, this phrase is of little or no use to communicate our love. Everyone has their well-entrenched understanding of the phrase and their listening is likely to filter your speaking. When you say, "I love you," are you truly heard and understood? Good luck!

## My thoughts:

### *I have love in my heart for you.*

Try this phrase when you have a physical sensation of love in your chest. This is a physically specific description and expression of love. Will your listener be able to really understand? Look them in the eye and touch your hand to your chest or, if it is appropriate to your relationship, take their hand and place it on your chest to let them know where the sensation of love resides.

## My thoughts:

## *My love is with you.*

Yes, we experience love in physical sensations. Yet love transcends space and time. We experience love in the present and it may be associated with the presence of a memory, a thought, or an event in the dreaming or planning stages, or an event in our history. Expressing, "my love is with you," lets the person for whom you express your love know that they are a source for your experience of love.

## My thoughts:

### *I see my love for you in all I do.*

Do you notice that your mood shows in all that you say and do? When you walk into a room, you contribute your mood to all others in that room. If you are joyful, others feel that joy. When you are angry, others feel that too. When you are filled with love, there is gentleness in your actions. When you are present to love for another, this shows up in how you conduct the activities of your everyday life. When you notice the impact of this love, share it with the person who so inspires you with love. Tell them, "I see my love for you in all I do."

## My thoughts:

## *When I hear your voice,*
## *love arises in my heart.*

Your brain and entire body store memories in the form of complex patterns. When we experience a pattern through our senses, our bodies (brain included) respond in a way consistent with how we have experienced that pattern before. If the current experience matches a portion of a larger experience, then we may re-experience the larger learned pattern in the present. For example, if when you are a child your mother sings you a happy song as she serves a delicious dinner, then hearing the same song as an adult may raise feelings of joy and hunger, even if it is early morning.

Telling your loved one "When I hear your voice, love arises in my heart," communicates the association their voice has for you. This tells them of their importance to you.

## My thoughts:

## *I have love for you.*

We tend to associate our experiences with a source that has a location and/or time associated with it. In telling another, "I have love for you," you take responsibility for being where the love resides in the present. You indicate that you "have" love. In this responsibility, you allow your loved one to be free to relate to your love in a manner of their choosing.

# My thoughts:

## *I see my love in you.*

With this phrase, you acknowledge your loved one as a source of your love or as an example of how you see your love expressed in the world.

When you recognize the actions, form, sound, smell, or touch of your loved one as a source of love for you, this is a phrase to use. You see your spouse interact with another with respect and compassion and this raises feelings of love. You can let your spouse know they are a source of love for you.

You have a favorite activity that brings you great joy and feelings of love. I use dancing as a simple example here, but it may be any activity or interest. When you see your boyfriend take joy in dancing, you delight in his joy. You recognize your love of dancing in him. You may express, "I see my love in you."

## My thoughts:

## *You are in my heart with my love.*

There is a great history of associating the emotion of love with the physical heart. Love emotions are often accompanied by sensations in the chest near the heart. Loving emotions may include the heart beating more quickly in excitement, or more calmly in comfort and safety.

As humans, we also have a history of relating to a non-physical sense of a personal center we refer to as the heart. We also use the word "heart" in this way to refer to the core, source, or most important aspect of a situation. We may say, "At the heart of the matter is ..."

When you say, "You are in my heart with my love," you are expressing that the effect and presence of another is resonant with your experience of yourself. You are telling them that you associate feelings of closeness, joy, and appreciation with their presence in your life.

## My thoughts:

### *Take my love with you.*

This is a way to offer your feelings to another for their experience. In saying, "Take my love with you," you are inviting the other to remember your love for them and your emotional connection to them.

## My thoughts:

## *You can count on my love to be here for you.*

This is a reassurance for your loved one. This is a way to re-presence them to your love and invite them to remember your love when they are away from you. If your friend is facing challenges in life that are accompanied with feelings of fear or uncertainty, this is a way you can tell them that your love is certain.

## My thoughts:

*You raise a feeling of love in my heart
that is as free and powerful as life itself.*

This is a way to express your love in a grand and, well... "gushy" manner. When expressing love, it is helpful to be clear in your communication and respectful of the listening that the other person has for you. This phrase might not go over well on a first date. It might serve you better with someone with whom you frequently have intimate conversations. When you use words such as "free and powerful" and "life itself" in this context, you might be inviting further discussion on what these words mean to you in the present context. Choose your words with the fullness of their meanings. Be responsible for the words you choose, or even the most eloquent phrases become exposed as empty and may be received as offensive.

## My thoughts:

## *I accept you completely with love.*

This is an expression of acceptance and forgiveness. Does someone doubt your love for them? Is this doubt a widening chasm between you and your loved one? Are you attaching your love for a person with their actions and the consequences of their actions? Such attachment denies the presence of love between you and your loved one.

Acceptance is different from approval. Acceptance and love travel together. Approval is a separate choice. Enjoy the presence of love, even in the absence of approval. This can heal your troubled relationships.

## My thoughts:

### *Keep my love with you when you are far away.*

This is a request that your loved one may accept or decline. In truth, your love is always with those to whom you give it. This request is an invitation for your loved one to remember your love and their connection to you. This request gives honor to the non-local nature of love—transcending time and space.

## My thoughts:

## *Believe in my love for you.*

This is a request for your loved one to reconsider any doubts they may have of the presence of your love. The request, "Believe in my love for you," challenges the attachment your loved one may hold between your love and a conflict between you and them. Truly, your love is always present and sometimes overlooked. Conflict arises and dissolves.

## My thoughts:

## *I send much love to you.*

Your love is a gift. Do you realize that your love is available for others even when your love is not in the focus of your attention? When you are aware of your love for another, it is available for them in an expanded way. When you say, "I send much love to you," your loved one is invited to bring their attention to your love in order to experience it in an expanded way.

## My thoughts:

## *You spark love in my heart with your smile.*

When you connect your experience of love with an action or characteristic of your loved one, you acknowledge a power they have in your life. When you acknowledge the power of another in one aspect of their life, you open their inquiry into the other aspects of their life and your love expands their awareness of their connection with the world. Be generous with your love.

## My thoughts:

## *Take my love. Everything else fades with time.*

Love is permanent beyond what you expect. Truly, love is eternal. Love is the canvas upon which time is painted. When you are aware of love, love is present. Love is present when you are forgetful of love. Love is omnipresent and always available for our attention. Are you willing to give your attention to love? How do you keep yourself present to love? How do you return your attention to love? One way you can turn your attention to love is to bring your love to the attention of others. While you are at it, bring attention to the timeless nature of love.

## My thoughts:

# Acknowledging Another's Love For You

Suppose for a while that the world is made of love and that all things from quark to supernova express patterns of love in the affinity of a perpetual dance. You experience love manifesting through you in your feelings, your words, and your actions. This manifestation is love's expression of itself.

You also see the expression of love in others. Sometimes you notice it when the other is not aware of the beauty of their words or actions. At times the other is consciously expressing their love and they are hungry for acknowledgement, acceptance, or reciprocation. Do you recall recognizing another's expression of love? Do you recall recognizing the love in another person's words or actions only many hours or days or years after the act of love?

These are opportunities to use words to acknowledge the love of another. There are many benefits available in the acknowledgement of love. The acknowledgement of love is a gift you give to the world. Such acknowledgement lets the person being acknowledged have the satisfaction that their efforts are received and impactful.

Notice that sometimes authentic expressions of love are accompanied by behaviors that are difficult to reconcile with love. For example, a guest at a dinner party may offer Loving help to wash the dishes and simultaneously complain about the food. These are simultaneous expressions that are not easily reconciled and may be completely independent. Acknowledging the Loving actions gives more energy and strength to the experience of love and leaves the complaints with less impact.

So, I encourage you to be generous with your acknowledgements of love. There is great power in acknowledgement to create a life experience of affinity, peace, and acceptance. No matter how much effort it takes for you to become comfortable and adept at acknowledging the expressions of love in others, the benefits are many times greater for you and for those you acknowledge.

## Internet Bonus!

David's suggestions for gifts when you want to acknowledge the love of another with more than words:

www.LittleBookOfBigLove.com/acknowledge

Share your expressions of love:

www.LittleBookOfBigLove.com/share

Get weekly tips on expressing and acknowledging love:

www.LittleBookOfBigLove.com/tips

## *I am present to your love.*

The power of love is awesome. When you are present to the love of another, and it is an appropriate setting, let them know it. When you acknowledge, "I am present to your love," you give responsibility to the other for their feelings of love. Notice that acknowledgement of the presence of love is not the same as agreement with the many meanings the other person might have attached to their feelings of love. Acknowledgement gives great space and freedom without attachments.

## My thoughts:

## *I am grateful for your love.*

This is a step beyond simple acknowledgement. This is an expression of gratitude, acceptance, and enjoyment. Your beloved may experience the power of their love inside of this acknowledgement.

## My thoughts:

### *Your love is in my heart.*

When you tell another, "Your love is in my heart," you communicate that the other's love is resonant with what is important and central to your life. More than acceptance, this is a way to verbally embrace the love of another.

**My thoughts:**

-----------------------------------------------------------

-----------------------------------------------------------

-----------------------------------------------------------

-----------------------------------------------------------

-----------------------------------------------------------

-----------------------------------------------------------

-----------------------------------------------------------

-----------------------------------------------------------

-----------------------------------------------------------

-----------------------------------------------------------

-----------------------------------------------------------

-----------------------------------------------------------

-----------------------------------------------------------

## *Your love is present in all you do.*

This acknowledgement of another and their love may be taken as an invitation to further discussion, so use it with care and authenticity. Respect the fullness of this phrase and reflect on how the specific actions of the other display their love.

## My thoughts:

## *Your love is with me always.*

To tell another, "Your love is with me always," tells them that you recognize the permanence of their love. Yes, love remains even when frustration, anger, and other emotions are present. Love does not disappear. When we are not feeling love, it is not that love is not present; it is that we are not present to love. If you take on expressing your love in this way, I invite you to be open to having your loved one remind you when you are not present to their love. Remember, love is always present.

## My thoughts:

## *When you touch me, I feel your love.*

Touch, sound, smell, actions, words, etc., may be great reminders of the presence of love. Acknowledge your loved one and bring to their attention when and how they bring love into your attention. Be responsible how your words invite further behaviors and embolden and invite your loved one to interact with you. There is great power in your speaking.

## My thoughts:

## *The love you give me is always with me.*

We experience love in many ways. Saying, "The love you give me is always with me," may be taken as an invitation to discuss the many ways you receive and experience love from the other. Consider that in saying this authentically, you hold in your mind specific ways in which you experience the love of the other person and how that shows up in your everyday life. In what ways does the remembrance of another's love impact your day?

## My thoughts:

*Your love is a shelter for me.*

We may recognize feelings of comfort, safety, warmth, or any of many sensations when we feel someone's love. When you identify such feelings, acknowledge this with your words. Acknowledgements can be received as an invitation for sustaining behaviors or ways of relating.

## My thoughts:

## *Your love refreshes my life.*

Recognize that your experience of another's love affects you in very specific ways. You may be affected emotionally, behaviorally, mentally, or psychologically. When you identify a way that is different for you in the presence of another's love than it would be if you were not present to that love, then acknowledge that impact. Acknowledgement cultivates your awareness of the love within yourself.

## My thoughts:

*Your love makes a difference
for everyone you touch.*

You see the impact of another's love on yourself and on others and you appreciate that impact. You want to see more of it. Acknowledging the impact on others nurtures that love and those who are impacted. Your acknowledgement is a contribution to the person you acknowledge and all who benefit. Be generous with your acknowledgement!

## My thoughts:

## *The love you give me rises from my every pore.*

Love cannot be observed directly in the same way time cannot be observed directly. Yet, as we have an experience of time indirectly through mechanical devices that follow principles of time and motion, we also have indirect ways to experience love. Such an abstraction of love is one reason love lends itself to poetic observation and interpretation. Certainly you do not look closely at your skin and see the steam of love rising. Still, you may feel sensations in your skin that are part of the pattern of your experience of love. Together with other sensations, you know that love exists and you are in the presence of love. Of course, just because your senses do not inform you of the presence of love at any given moment, that does not mean that love is not present.

## My thoughts:

## *Your love is a light to the shadows of my fears.*

This is a mix of acknowledgment of emotional effect and metaphor. Of course, you may say this to whomever you like. As for me, I reserve expressions like this for people I have an established relationship with. For me, this is an intimate expression I imagine being more appropriate for acknowledging a family member who consoles me through a painful event and less appropriate for someone I meet at a party.

## My thoughts:

## *Your love comforts me.*

Many people offer you comfort throughout life. Comfort may come from friends, strangers, family members, teachers, coworkers, or professionals. The source of offers of true comfort is love, which manifests as compassion. Acknowledging love as the source honors the most sublime aspect of human nature. When you bring attention to the source of compassion, you hold open a pathway for that love to continue to flow into manifestation in thought, word, and deed.

**My thoughts:**

## *I am nourished by your love.*

This is a direct recognition of you as a beneficiary of the love of another. It is going beyond acknowledging that love is present, recognizing that love gives you strength and vitality. The recognition of nourishment leads to the understanding that the love we receive becomes our own love that shows in our lives and the love we give to others.

**My thoughts:**

*Wherever I am, your love is with me.*

Yes, go ahead and let the person who loves you know that you are present to that love wherever you might go. Give the person who loves you the experience that their love transcends time and distance.

## My thoughts:

*All loneliness fades when you approach me and touch me with love.*

Here is another example of how to let the person who loves you know that their acts of love impact you in specific ways. In this way you not only acknowledge their power and impact in your life, you also let them know a way in which you receive and benefit from their love.

## My thoughts:

## *Although you are gone, your love continues to grow within me.*

This is a way to acknowledge love you have from someone who has moved a great distance away. It is also a way to acknowledge the impact on you of the love of a deceased person. Once you receive love, you are never the same again. Love takes root inside you and shifts your personal development. The impact within you continues whether your loved one is near or far or if their body is breathing or not. Love does not have the restrictions of a physical body. When you give love, it lives on.

## My thoughts:

*Your love gives me courage to see
my strength and worthiness.*

Wow! You notice the big contribution the people in your life are to you. With their love, you notice that you have courage, strength, and worthiness. What else do you notice? Yes, all these qualities are always within you. Sometimes, however, you do not notice them. You might even think you do not have them at all. When the people who give you their love recognize your great qualities, those qualities somehow seem more accessible to you. When this happens, acknowledge the people who give you their love. Then, give your love to another who will benefit.

## My thoughts:

## *My life is better because of you and the love you give.*

This is one way to get to the point. While sometimes specifics are beautiful, there are times when painting a broader landscape is impactful. Generously acknowledge the broad effect of the contribution others are to you. In doing so, allow yourself to see the broad impact of your own sharing of love. Yes, your love makes lives better. Yes, your life is better from the love others give to you.

## My thoughts:

### *Thank you for loving me.*

There are times when you are easy to love. There are also times when you are not so easy to love. Those who have love for you do not withhold their love when you are difficult. If it seems like that, consider the ways in which you may be thwarting the delivery of love. Let go of your resistance. When you find that someone is loving you while you resist and deny that love, acknowledge them in this simple and beautiful way.

## My thoughts:

## *I feel loved.*

Let the people who love you know that the message is getting through. Remind yourself that you are feeling the love now. Know that this feeling is always available because love is always present, even when you are distracted by other feelings, emotions, and circumstances.

## My thoughts:

# Acknowledging Mutual Love

If the Universe is a manifestation or an expression of love, then it makes perfect sense that love may be experienced at any time, in any place, under any circumstance. One of the favorite situations in which people seek to experience love is in the company of another person. Do you gauge the quality of your relationships by the intensity of your experience of love? Is the difference between acquaintance, friend, and lover one of degree of affinity or love?

Love is present in every relationship. I suggest that the quality of a relationship is a measure of how present the parties in the relationship are to the love that is ever-present. Do you get that? Love is always present. We experience love when we are present to the love. There are many tools we can use to become present to love. We can recognize love in a blood relationship to our family members. You can find affinity with a classmate or someone who is born in the same town as you. You may choose to believe that it is easier to share love with a being of your own species... or not. Really, the measure of relationship and affinity is arbitrary. The love is ubiquitous.

When you find it difficult to acknowledge the love between you and another, it is likely that you are being distracted by the differences present. Distracted by differences, affinity is not getting the attention that can bring a greater experience of love. So, practice acknowledging the presence of mutual love when it is readily available and easy to do. These times are often called, "the good times." Later, when you are adept at acknowledging love during "the good times", you are in a stronger position to recognize and acknowledge mutual love during "difficult times." Conflict can be disrupted by moving attention from differences to the mutual love that is present before and remains after any period of conflict.

Embrace the presence of mutual love and experience the embrace of love around you.

## Internet Bonus!

David's suggestions for gifts when you want to acknowledge mutual love of another with more than words:

`www.LittleBookOfBigLove.com/sharelove`

Share your expressions of love:

`www.LittleBookOfBigLove.com/share`

Get weekly tips on expressing and acknowledging love:

`www.LittleBookOfBigLove.com/tips`

**My thoughts:**

### *I am present to love with you.*

Is this an acknowledgement of love that exists when you are with the other person or is it an acknowledgement of love that is with the other person always? Yes! It is either and both. Such is the pervasive nature of love. Any way you look at it, it is all made of love.

## My thoughts:

*When you are gone, your love remains with me, and my love remains with you.*

You and your loved one each experience the commitment that the other has a great life. This commitment does not diminish with distance or time. This is a way to recognize the transcendence of love.

## My thoughts:

*There is only one love and*
*we reside in it together.*

As human beings we are able to experience life from many perspectives. The shifting of perspectives is a beautiful dance between perception and reality. Every perspective offers its own usefulness and its own limitations. There is a perspective that you have a love to give for me to receive and that I have a separate love to give for you to receive. This is an amazing illusion! Love is the canvas upon which time is painted. Enjoy every color while knowing it is one illustration.

## My thoughts:

## *The life we live together is a product of our love.*

The simple and gross form of the word "together" relates to spatial proximity. Spatial proximity is rather dull absent the awareness of mutual interaction. On a more subtle level, we are together within time, regardless of relative proximity. Still more subtle is our togetherness without spatial and temporal reference. In the most subtle truth, we are together as one.

While this may be interesting and moving, what does it teach us for our everyday life? The thread that binds us together is love. When you live as a person and share your life with other persons, you recognize that togetherness in relation to the level of your recognition of love between you and others. The more that love is mutually recognized between you and another, the greater is the experience of joy in everyday life. So, try acknowledging the impact of mutual love in your life.

## My thoughts:

## *My love resides in your heart*

This is an intimate conversation. Your heart is the core of your being. Your heart is your nature. When you recognize that your love resides in the heart of another, you are recognizing the common humanity you share with that person. This conversation takes a willingness to be vulnerable. Enjoy! You have my blessings.

## My thoughts:

## *Love is here when we are together.*

This is not to say that love is not present when you and your loved one are not together. Rather this affirms the presence of love. Even though love transcends time and space, proximity in time and space can help us experience and celebrate love more vividly. So, take a moment and acknowledge the presence of love and celebrate!

## My thoughts:

*When your eyes sparkle and your smile beams, I know the love in our friendship.*

Notice the specific ways in which love manifests in your friendships. Acknowledge these signs to your friend. Bringing these signs to the attention of your friend gives them another access to the joy of love in a friendship.

## My thoughts:

## *Our friendship has a love without rival. I am here for you.*

Love and romance are not dependent upon each other. Love in friendship is pure, steady, and dependable. Honor the depth of love that you share with your friends. Recognize that when you are with your friend, in the love of friendship, that you and your friend can transcend any challenge and experience the greatness and joy of life.

## My thoughts:

*The love in our friendship is my companion when you are away.*

Companionship resides in love. When physical distance separates you from your friend, the companionship is still available in your mutual love. When you express this to your friend, you both become more aware of the subtle gifts of friendship.

## My thoughts:

*Our love is the same love that fills the Universe; it is with us always.*

You have heard it before: there is only one love. We all experience it through the portal of our own lives. So, should we be surprised when we have such different experiences of this one love? When your vision of love is clear and you experience its universal nature, share that experience with those you are near to. When they are distracted from the Universal Love, remind them it is present, awaiting their attention.

## My thoughts:

*There is one love in the entire universe.*
*We experience this together.*

This phrase draws attention to the universally connecting aspect of love. In a subtle sense, this phrase is redundant in that it restates our togetherness after recognizing the unity of the universe. Still, the reminder is powerful and helpful because of our human tendency to be distracted from our interdependence and common humanity. Yes! We experience Universal Love together.

## My thoughts:

### *Your love is my love.*

When you notice that your loved one is relating to their love as a personal and private experience, not shared by another, this is one way to bring their attention to that their love is shared by you. Truly, love is only experienced in sharing.

## My thoughts:

# Resources

For more tips on expressing and acknowledging love, visit:

`www.LittleBookOfBigLove.com/tips`

For David's gift suggestions visit:

`www.LittleBookOfBigLove.com/gifts`

For holistic resources on healthy living and healing, visit:

`www.holistic.com`

For training in living a life you love and living it powerfully, go to The Landmark Forum:

http://landmarkforum.com

# LEARN MORE!

David's speaking calendar is available on:

http://www.JoyIsAvailable.com

You can read more of his writings on his blog:

http://blog.JoyIsAvailable.com

For training in living a life you love and living
it powerfully, go to The Landmark Forum:

http://landmarkforum.com